# A SHORT AND SWEET
## History of the Chemung Valley
from the Iroquois days to 1923

by Dr. Arthur W. Booth

William C. Gill

William H. Arnold

*A Short and Sweet History of the Chemung Valley from the Iroquois Days to 1923* by Dr. Arthur W. Booth, William C. Gill, and William H. Arnold. This version edited by New York History Review.

Copyright ©2019 New York History Review. Some rights reserved.

ISBN: 978-1-950822-07-2

First Edition

Printed in the United States of America

*Dedicated to the three gentlemen who wrote these histories for the Elmira Historical Pageant, giving Elmira the impetus to start the Chemung County Historical Society in 1923.*

MAJOR GENERAL JOHN SULLIVAN,
A distinguish'd OFFICER in the CONTINENTAL ARMY.

# Table of Contents

The Iroquois..................................................................9

General John Sullivan's Expedition............................15

Historical Outline............................................................23

Early Settlers in the Chemung Valley............................33

The first Sullivan's Monument circa 1911 before it fell down.

## The Iroquois
### By Dr. Arthur W. Booth, Elmira, New York

The early European navigators landed on our Atlantic coast, at infrequent intervals between the tenth and fifteenth centuries. Upon arriving, they encountered a hitherto unknown type of red-skinned man, the American Indian or Amerind. Ten thousand years of human culture separated them, for the Amerinds were still living in the Stone Age.

Just how or when these Amerinds arrived in America is, of course, not known. They are supposed to be off-shoots of the great Mongol race of Asia and to have entered our continent across the stepping-stones formed by the innumerable islands lying between Siberia and Alaska. Judging by their wide variation in type and language, there were no doubt several distinct waves of immigration. The general distribution over the entire country suggests, they had lived in America from the very dawn of history.

It is of absorbing interest to observe how the aboriginal races of America were living and working out their social destinies. They were uninfluenced by any contact, with the world's advancing civilization elsewhere.

Of all the distinct tribes occupying the upper and eastern portions of what is now the United States, the Iroquois nation was without question the most intelligent, and powerful.

The confederation of five nations - the Mohawks, Onondagas, Oneidas, Senecas, and Cayugas, to which later the Tuscaroras were joined all closely allied by blood ties and community interests.

According to tradition, they sprang from the great Dakota tribe. They had gradually won their way east by six centuries of encounter and conquest. They had arrived in central New York at a period just preceding the colonization of Canada and New England by the white man.

Here, they controlled the vast area between the St. Lawrence River, the Potomac River, the Hudson Valley, and Ohio.

At the height of their power, it is estimated, that they numbered from twenty-five to seventy-five thousand, besides many tribes who could be called upon for assistance in time of need.

Unlike most of the Amerinds, they ceased their nomadic habits and had established permanent villages about the central New York lakes and along the beautiful streams and river valleys. Well-worn trails connected the communities and led from the Great Lakes to the Hudson, Susquehanna, Delaware and Ohio Rivers. Our railways and state roads now follow these identical paths. Many of our towns and cities are built on the sites of the former Iroquois villages.

As with all primitive people, they lived close to nature from, whose bounty they derived their sustenance in the way of game and fish, and the edible vegetables indigenous to the country. Besides these, we know that the Iroquois cultivated cleared ground, raising corn in abundance, beans, squash, pumpkin, and tobacco.

The early Jesuits brought them improved varieties of apple, pear, plum, and peach.

Their villages consisted of rectangular houses built of elm tree bark supported on a framework of heavy poles. Several families, closely related, occupied a single structure. The house was long with a central aisle, flanked by built-in bunks, not unlike the Pullman sleeping car arrangement. An ample hole in the roof met the white fathers in conference, breathed the loftiest sentiments of con1mon brotherhood of man. Appeals too often addressed to minds narrowed and cramped by religious bigotry and bent only upon political aggrandizement and territorial conquest.

Their religion was a natural and straightforward belief in a Creator, the Great Spirit - faith without the element of fear or dread of future punishment and with only the vaguest of ideas of a next life and reward. There was no priestcraft, and they pursued no religious exercises.

Their code of morals was all that could be desired. They respected their neighbor's wife, property, and rights. Personal chastity was proverbial in marked contrast to aboriginal types in general. Marriages were monogamous. They had perfected a system against consanguineous unions, anticipating modern eugenic principles.

Their government was a real democracy in which the women had an equal voice with the men at their councils. Whenever any great undertaking was proposed, affecting the entire League, it was not executed unless all of the component nations agreed. Each nation still had its separate autonomy, very much after the present plan in these United States. All in all, we behold a most remarkable resemblance to the political development worked out here in later years by the Anglo-Saxon race.

What might the outcome have been if there been no interruption or interference by the Europeans? The substantial growth of social ideas; the high standards of human conduct; the broad conceptions of common humanity; the remarkable skill of their artisans suggests exciting speculations as to the ultimate culture of these children of the forest. Europeans brought them firearms and rum; confused their religious ideas; treated them with the greatest injustice; taught them to cheat at trade, and finally drove them ruthlessly from their age-long ancestral homeland.

Joseph Brant [Thayendanegea] as painted by George Romney in 1776.

# General John Sullivan's Expedition of 1779

## By Dr. Arthur W. Booth, Elmira, NY

A tall granite shaft stands on the crest of a high hill overlooking the Chemung Valley, four miles below the city of Elmira, New York. Erected by the State of New York in 1911, the monument commemorates the Battle of Newtown which occurred on Sunday, August 29, 1779.

Near here, General John Sullivan's army fought Joseph Brant (Thayendanegea). Sullivan lead an army of 5000 men. Brant had gathered his warriors, along with 500 British soldiers to halt Sullivan's invasion into the Iroquois homeland.

The early Revolutionary War writers gave scant mention to this engagement. Subsequent historians have utterly failed to grasp the importance, not only of this particular battle but of the entire campaign.

This expedition consisted of a problematic march of 280 miles through unsurveyed forests. Part of the travel over mountainous wastes; the crossing and re-crossing of swift and impetuous watercourses, until at last, late in the Fall, the army marched triumphantly through the garden spot of the New World - the lake country of central New York, and on beyond into the broad Genesee Valley.

Keep in mind that this country was hitherto unknown to the white man. Washington anticipated the necessity of this invasion and had been quietly collecting all possible data from trappers, voyageurs, friendly Indians, and British deserters. But much of this information was inaccurate and extremely vague. Sullivan's march was of necessity, then, a voyage of discovery as well as destruction. He was sent into an unknown country to destroying a foe whose numbers and strength was likewise unknown. The territory to be invaded comprised all of what is now the upper half of Pennsylvania and all of New York State west of the Hudson River.

Owing to the unwise treatment of the Indians by the Canadian French, the English had long ago won their friendship and alliance. Sir William Johnson of upper New York, had, by his tactful management of Indian affairs, established great influence over them. Sir William died before the Revolution broke out, but his power so endured that his successors had no difficulty in persuading the Indians to take up arms against the revolting colonists. Unfortunately, they fell under the leadership of the Butlers and MacDonalds. Their savagery far exceeded the skill of the Indians. The Butlers incited the Indians to the massacres of Wyoming in Pennsylvania, and Cherry Valley, and other settlements in New York.

In addition to the continued raids upon our border settlements and the material aid rendered by the Indians in many battles, their fertile gardens throughout central New York were furnishing abundant food to the regular British troops along the seaboard.

Realizing these conditions, Washington and his advisors became convinced of the dire necessity of destroying the Iroquois and his home. Early in 1779, Congress authorized Washington to send an expedition into the Iroquois country for this purpose.

Washington planned this campaign with consummate skill, and so timed the march that Sullivan's men would arrive in the rich agricultural country during the early harvest. His orders were, "The immediate objects are the destruction and devastation of their settlements and the capture of as many prisoners of every age and sex as possible. It will be essential to ruin their crops now in the ground and prevent their planting more." Sullivan was to start from Easton, Pennsylvania. Then cross over the high mountainous divide of the Pocono Plateau into the Susquehanna Valley. Here they were to be joined by other troops from southern Pennsylvania at Wyoming, and then proceed up the Susquehanna river to Tioga Point (now Athens, Pennsylvania).

General James Clinton was to start from the Mohawk Valley. Then to cross over to Otsego Lake, and follow down the north branch of the Susquehanna and join Sullivan at

Red Jacket, Seneca War Chief. Chromolithograph by Corbould from a painting by C.B. King; printed by C. Hallmandel.

Tioga Point - destroying as he went. The combined armies were then to proceed north into the Iroquois country of central and western New York. Finally, to advance to Fort Erie, near Niagara, to destroy that stronghold which the British had erected. Meanwhile, Colonel Daniel Brodhead was ordered to proceed with 600 men up the Allegheny River from Fort Pitt, now Pittsburgh with a view of joining Sullivan somewhere along the Genesee Valley. Brodhead's march devastated the Indian towns along the river. Owing to sickness among his troops and inadequate army supplies, Brodhead was obliged to return without meeting Sullivan. He had only advanced so far as what is now the southern boundary of New York State.

On August 26, Sullivan, having been joined by Clinton, started his army northward, taking the route up the Chemung River. About 16 miles up this stream was a little Indian village called Newtown, which they reached on the 29th. Here the advance scouts discovered breastworks extending for about half a mile on a ridge - protected by a high hill behind, a large creek at the left and front, and the Chemung River on the right. The great Mohawk chief, Joseph Brant, commanded his warriors who were entrenched in this position. Colonel Guy Johnson, with Captains Walter Butler and MacDonald commanding 500 regular British troops, were placed on a neighboring ridge to guard Brant's right flank.

After Sullivan had ascertained this defense, he dispatched two regiments by a circuitous route to attack the enemy's left flank and rear. He also sent a detachment around to the enemy's right side, meanwhile keeping up a mild frontal attack to engage the attention of the enemy and divert him from the flanking movements. A prearranged plan at the end of two hours included a simultaneous attack on both flanks and in front. The firing of a cannon was to be the signal for attack. When this signal came, the men sent to the left side were still floundering in a swampy thicket, but eventually, they gained higher ground though much exhausted. Here the hardest fighting occurred, which for a time, boded disaster to the colonists, but the persistent crash of artillery had at last shattered the morale of the Indians and Brant sounded the alarm for a retreat. The Indians fled northward and scattered over the wide valley and up among the surrounding hills. Sullivan's campaign made its last definite stand and direct engagement here.

He now began a systematic destruction of the villages and fields in the vicinity of the battle, after which he moved his men northward towards Seneca Lake destroying all in his path. The Indians kept up their retreat - always far ahead of Sullivan's advance, picking up the women and children as they proceeded.

Sullivan marched his army along the east bank of Seneca Lake, crossed over the head of the lake to where now stands

Geneva, and where there was at that time a populous Indian village. He then went to Canandaigua and thence to Genesee Castle, the Capitol of the Indian confederation. Owing to his dwindling supplies, the lateness of the season and the failure of Brodhead to join him at this point, Sullivan decided to retrace his steps back into Pennsylvania. He had destroyed 40 villages, thousands of bushels of harvested corn, countless orchards, and all standing crops. The Iroquois civilization was a smoking ruin.

The Indian refugees were quartered in barracks at Fort Erie that winter, which was an exceptionally severe one, and many of them died from exposure and scurvy.

Sullivan arrived at Fort Reed, now Elmira, one month from the date of his battle, and taking boats, descended the river where his troops dispersed later into military camps. His total loss of men was only 41, most extraordinary under the circumstances.

Sullivan did not accomplish all that he was sent out to do. Considering the well-nigh insuperable difficulties and obstacles, one cannot but declare the prodigious task was still well performed. This expedition removed a powerful ally of the British. It also rendered untenable a possible path through which the English might descend from Canada to attack the mid-Atlantic colonies.

Sullivan's men comprised troops from Connecticut, Massachusetts, Vermont, New York, Pennsylvania, New Jersey, and Virginia. To move this expedition, he had two hundred and fourteen boats and 1200 horses. Unscrupulous army contractors left his men were improperly clothed, fed and equipped. The army foraged for its food for most of the trip and suffered greatly from lack of shoes and clothing.

After the declaration of peace, many of Sullivan's soldiers returning to their homes became restless under the quiet and restraint of the east. They saw the beginning of migrating settlers going west and retraced their steps to the fertile valleys of central New York. They came this time, not for conquest, but to subdue the soil and erect homesteads. Throughout central and western New York, there is scarcely a family or a deed of the property, which cannot be traced back in some branch or way to Sullivan's men.

## Historical Outline
### by William C. Gill

For the sake of comparison, let us visualize. It was not until 1828 that the village of Newtown changed its name to Elmira. In 1836 Chemung County was established by dividing Tioga County. In 1823 the state was paying a reward of $5 each for the destruction of any wolf or wolf--whelp or panther, and $2 each for wild cats in Tioga County. The preceding paragraph ought to make it easier to comprehend the panorama as the story unfolds.

Many of the early settlers were men who had observed the valley in 1779 while traveling with General Sullivan's army. In 1786 General James Clinton, who had commanded a brigade in the battle of Newtown. General John Hathorn and John Cantine were appointed Commissioners to survey the lands of the county. Settlers bought property at eighteen pence an acre.

Settlements commenced in 1786, and the more significant portion of the pioneers was here by 1792. Many emigrated from Orange County and the counties of Northampton, Pennsylvania, and Sussex, New Jersey. Also came families that had initially located near Wyoming, Pennsylvania, under the Connecticut title. The Wyoming group had been ejected by

Pennsylvania who asserted the claim of William Penn to the land in controversy.

When the white pioneers came to erect their abodes here, there were Indians between the Chemung River and Seneca Lake. The territory was a common hunting ground. Two score of Indian families had cabins near the present Wisner Park. There was a second Indian village on the flats near the junction of Newtown Creek and the Chemung River. A third village was located on the east side of Newtown Creek their cabins dotting the land between that point and the hill at the foot of the present Gleason Sanitarium. In 1804, smallpox broke out among the Indians. They may have believed it an evil omen for they shortly picked up their chattels and joined fellow tribesmen near Batavia.

The original village of civilized, whites were laid out on a plot of land granted to Jeffrey Wisner on Newtown Creek and first buildings were erected about 1790 on what is now Sullivan Street. Within a few years, about 1796, a courthouse and jail were built on the east side of Sullivan Street just north of Church Street. It was a building of sawn logs, the lower part being used as a jail and dwelling for the jailer: the second floor as a courtroom and place of public worship: the third floor or attic as a temple for Union Lodge. F. and A. M. beginning on August 26. 1793. That place served for a jail and courthouse a long time. In 1824 a more modern building was erected on

Old log cabin courthouse and first Masonic Temple on Sullivan Street in Newtown/Elmira.

Lake Street near the site of the present courthouse. In 1862 the current courthouse was constructed. The 1824 building was moved to the present site of the Elks' Club on Market Street and served as the "City Hall" until 1896 when the current artistic municipal building was dedicated. Note that 100 years ago, our ancestors were using the Sullivan Street Court House. To supply pure water for the jail, Court House and Masonic Lodge.

He was a colonel and judge; also engaged in trade with John Jacob Astor. About 1792, Captain Daniel McDowell took charge of the store. Other early merchants were Guy Maxwell, Thomas M. Perry, James Irwin, Michael Pfantz, Ephraim Heller, Lyman, Robert and Miles Covell, Isaac Baldwin, John Cherry, Thomas, and Samuel Maxwell and Isaac Reynolds.

Robert Covell opened a general business in Elmira in 1807. For many years the Covells were leading figures in the community. In 1819, John Arnot established a business in Elmira. He became a foremost factor in the progress of his chosen home. He was one of the founders and the second president of the Chemung Canal Bank. Also, in 1819 there was established the first stage route between Elmira and Wilkes-Barre. It carried the mail as well as express and passengers and resembled the stagecoach of later days in the far west.

Indeed, the early days of Elmira were much like the pioneer period of most frontier towns. Horse racing prevailed on

Sunday and distilleries were more numerous than churches. For all that, the pioneers were temperate people.

The first Post Office was established January 1, 1801, with Aaron Konkle as postmaster. George M. Diven, present postmaster of Elmira, at his office has a complete list of, all the postmasters serving here and the original signature of most of them.

In 1792 the first sawmill was erected by Abner and Henry Wells at Wellsburg. For many years the main products of Chemung County were agriculture and lumber. As late as 40 years ago it was common to see oxen drawing logs to the sawmills at Elmira. The Arnot Mill on William Street was the last to respond to the demand for log sawing.

In 1815 the first newspaper was established by Brindle and Murphy and called *The Telegraph*. Although we had no electric telegraph in those days, Thomas Maxwell, lawyer, Congressman, and County historian, is authority relative to the first paper. Ausburn Towner, another historian, credits *The Investigator* as the first paper. However, that was not instituted until 1820 by Job Smith. According to Mr. Maxwell - who ought to have known *The Investigator* was changed to *The Tioga Register* in 1822 and to *The Elmira Gazette* in 1828. However, the Elmira *Star-Gazette* doesn't claim its origin in 1820, but owns up to 1828 as its birth year. Elmira has been blessed abundantly in the standard of its newspapers. With the church

The Chemung Canal ran through the middle of Elmira. This photo circa 1870, taken by Elisha VanAken.

and the school, the press has always sought to make Elmira a worthwhile community.

The first school built of logs came in 1798, while the first clergyman to come among the early settlers was the Rev. Daniel Thatcher, a Presbyterian, who arrived in 1798.

Many sheep were raised in the county; hence, woolen factories became a requisite. It was difficult to transport virgin wool in those days. The first woolen mill was established in 1820 in Southport by Silas Billings. The last was the mill of Daniel and Ransom Pratt, founders of the Second National Bank, located on East Avenue near the Creek and now used as a Knitting Mill for cotton. It flourished until about thirty years ago. Flour mills were also numerous. The pioneers floated their wheat down the river to Wilkes-Barre to be ground. Gradually small mills were established. In 1828 Samuel Hotchkin built a dam across the Chemung and erected a flour mill near College Avenue, then designated Mill Street. That mill was razed within the past decade. In 1836 the Arnot Mills and Creek dam were erected at the foot of East Water Street. That mill still stands.

Facilities for communication took a great stride for those days when, on April 15, 1829, the state legislature appropriated $300,000 for a canal from the Chemung River to Seneca Lake. Work was begun in 1830. Colonel John Hendy "Elmira's first citizen" as he was lovingly designated - threw the first spadeful of dirt on what is now State Street. In 1832 it was completed. There was a grand celebration at Elmira as the first boat drawn by four horses proceeded towards Seneca Lake, decorated by American flags. Colonel Hendy occupied the place of honor.

Stagecoaches for a long time continued the leading passenger carrying routes while canal boats conveyed freight.

In the Fall of 1849, the Erie Railroad was completed to Elmira. The same year illuminating gas was introduced here; hence, we progressed doubly. In 1853 another railroad was started connecting Elmira and Williamsport and, ten years later, was extended to Canandaigua. It is now a part of the Pennsylvania System.

In 1876 the Utica, Ithaca and Elmira Railroad was built. That is now a branch of the Lehigh Valley. The same year the Elmira and State Line Railroad was completed to Blossburg, Pennsylvania. In 1882 it was sold to the Erie railroad company. In 1882, on April 3, the first passenger train on the Delaware, Lackawanna and Western railroad reached the small wooden station at Elmira. Subsequently, the Lackawanna extended its line to Buffalo. Few cities possess advantages attached to Elmira as a railroad center. Thousands of railroad men reside here. Its railroads provide convenient transportation to all parts of the country.

Following the advent of the first railroad, Elmira began to multiply. Brilliant lawyers and skilled doctors located here.

In 1855 there was established Elmira College, the first institution in the world exclusively for women authorized to grant degrees to women equal to men. In 1858, the Young Men's Christian Association was instituted. The following year the Elmira Board of Education was organized. In 1861 Elmira became a military rendezvous. In 1864 a rebel prison camp was established here. The same year, April 7, 1864, Elmira became a city

During 1864 Elmira had a population of approximately 13,000, and the entire county had 27,000. Real estate and personal property for the whole county during 1864 assessed at $7,238,709.

Much might be said of our public men, fraternities, civic organization, Churches and schools, notable political gatherings and contests. But space forbids. The previous is but a brief outline, yet it should imbue in those who read it a spirit of research.

Thomas Maxwell, who was born at Athens, Pennsylvania in 1792 and came to Elmira in 1796 with his parents, wrote a history of the valley in 1863. A second history appeared in 1868 written by Andrew B. Galatian who was City Editor of the *Gazette* during the Civil War. Mr. Galatian secured much additional information from Mr. Maxwell. In 1892 Ausburn Towner compiled the most extended history to that point of this valley although there is a true history of

Chemung and four other counties extant and published in the late 1870s. It covers Chemung County remarkably well. In 1894 the writer of this article at the solicitation of Clay W. Holmes wrote a 20,000-word history. Within the past decade, Mr. Holmes wrote a very complete book of Elmira during the Civil War period.

***What we need today is a Chemung County Historical Society. May it have its inception through the force of the Elmira Historic Pageant of 1923.***

## The Early Settlers and how they came to the Chemung Valley
### by William H. Arnold, Local Historian

From the beautiful Chemung Valley, 1923 looks back to 1788, one hundred and forty-five years, and sees a land upon which no white man had ever lived. On the site of our prosperous city, the wild deer roamed undisturbed save by the aboriginals of the forest. The great Ganundasaga trail passed northerly from Tioga Point and Chemung. It skirted the hills on the east of the then Tioga River, through the valley leading through to Seneca Lake. Then it continued along the west side of the lake until it reached Kanadesaga and Ganundagua. From there, it went west to Niagara, though the most frequented route from the Susquehanna was by way of the valley of the Canisteo.

All of this happened before Major General John Sullivan, with his army made his historic march. Sullivan intended to punish the Iroquois Nation for atrocities of the past and to make desolate the fertile lands of the lake region.

The first white settler, where now stands the city of Elmira, was Captain John Hendy, a soldier of the Revolution, who fought under Washington at Princeton, Trenton, and Monmouth. Accompanying him was a small boy named

Dan Hill. They came up the river in a canoe from Tioga Point, where the Captain had left his family. They landed at Newtown point, a junction of the Tioga (now Chemung) River and Spring Creek (Newtown Creek). There they erected a shelter of saplings and bark and here was planted the first field of corn by a white man in the valley. The site of this hut was at the foot of what is now Water Street.

In the Fall of the same year, he brought his family here from Tioga Point and moved further up the river. to a site opposite Roricks' Glen, where he resided until his death. All that remains of the cabin, which was his home for so many years, is the ruin of the fireplace, and this is fast crumbling away.

When Captain Hendy arrived in the valley there were three Indian villages within what is now the city limits. One was situated on Main street near what is now Wisner Park, which consisted of some thirty or forty wigwams. Another was on the flats near Newtown Creek, while still another was on the east side of the creek near the foot of "Watercure Hill."

The names of the actual settlers in the valley previous to 1788, included the following: William Wynkoop, Isaac McBride, William Buck and his son Elijah, Daniel McDowel (now spelled McDowell), Charles Emmit, Israel Parsloe (now Parshall), Uzual Bates, Solomon Bennett, Elijah Grissell (now Griswold), Gideon Gris sell. Roger Conant, John Spaulding, Thomas Baldwin, Uriah Stevens, John Stevens, Joel Thomas, Anthony Rummerfield, Nathan Van Auken, Isaac Terwilliger, Josiah Green, Abijah Batterson, John Squires, Ebenezer Green, Green Bentley, Christian Mynier, win, Abner Kelsey, Elisha Brown, William Wilder, Stephen Kent, John Suffern, Stephen Gardner, Solomon Lane, Lebeus Hammond, Abraham Miller, Samuel Tubbs, Benjamin Clark, Jabez Culver, Jared Stull, George Hill, William Jenkins, Cornelius Westfall, Walter Waters, John Jay Achmuty, Jonas Bellow, John Hendy, Christian Mynier, Tunis Dolson, John Morris and John Miller.

Many of these settlers were men who had accompanied the Sullivan Expedition into the Lake country in 17i9 and thus became acquainted with the productiveness of the lands of the valley. Following the expedition, and the return to their homes, they told wonderful tales of the land where the corn grew in stalks to the height of sixteen feet and the ears were a foot-and-a-half long, and every kind of vegetable in proportion, including watermelons and pumpkins.

The settlers were nearly all from near Wyoming, one of them or their immediate ancestors came from Connecticut or from Orange County.

Practically the only route of travel was by way of the river. The road which had been used by Sullivan's army a few years before had long grown over, and permitted but a hard, laborious way of getting into the valley. The river furnished a more comfortable and satisfactory way. It was by this courage that the majority of the pioneers came, bringing their families and their worldly goods to their newly chosen homes. They came in boats or in canoes, which were propelled by paddles or long poles, making a long tiresome journey. Sometimes it necessitated many trips before they had what they termed comforts of home, which we know not of today.

John Sly, who settled on the south side of the river, erecting a log house in today's Brand Park, came to the valley in 1788. He brought his young wife on horseback, both riding the same horse.

Up to 1807, there was no route except the river route between Newtown and Tioga Point. About that time a trail or road was made on either side of the river between these points. It gave access to the valley when the river was not navigable.

The pioneers were men of high energy; stalwart men every one. Very few of the present generation can appreciate the trials and sufferings of these hardy pioneers or what they gave up in leaving the settlements from which they came. Every comfort had surrounded them. Schools were abundant, and the sound of the church bells familiar to the ear. They arrived to face the privations in forming a new settlement in a wilderness, inhabited by wild beasts or the more terrible red men.

It was from such families as these that came those who had so much to do in the building up of a community that was destined to become the beautiful and progressive city, which we are pleased to call home.

Verily, they built better than they knew.

# More Chemung County books from New York History Review

www.NewYorkHistoryReview.com

*Penal Ordinances of Elmira, New York 1899*

*Zim's Foolish History of Elmira*

*Historical Sketch of the Chemung Valley New York*

*Queen City Adventure*

*Souvenir of Elmira*

*Storefronts Elmira, New York*

*The Great Inter-State Fair in Elmira, New York*

*Elmira Academy of Sciences*

*A Brief History of Chemung County*

www.ingramcontent.com/pod-product-compliance
Lightning Source LLC
Chambersburg PA
CBHW031439040426
42444CB00006B/887